Contents

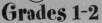

About
Writing Centers
Grades 1-2

What's Great About This Book

Centers are a wonderful, fun way for students to practice important skills. The 13 centers in this book are self-contained and portable. Students may work at a desk, at a table, or even on the floor. Once you've made the centers, they're ready to use any time.

What's in This Book

The teacher directions page includes how to make the center and a description of the student task

Full-color materials needed for the center

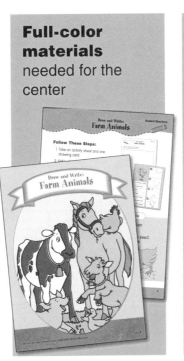

Reproducible activity sheets to practice and evaluate writing skills

Portfolio cover and a student center checklist

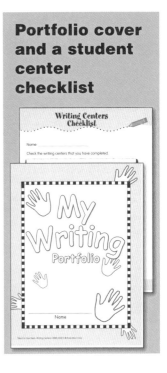

How to Use the Centers

The centers are intended for skill practice, not to introduce skills. It is important to model the use of each center before students do the task independently.

Questions to Consider:

- Will students select a center, or will you assign the centers?
- Will there be a specific block of time for centers, or will the centers be used throughout the day?
- Where will you place the centers for easy access by students?
- What procedure will students use when they need help with the center tasks?
- How will you track the tasks and centers completed by each student?

Making a File Folder Center

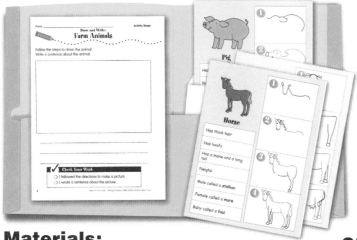

Folder centers are easily stored in a box or file crate. Students take a folder to their desks to complete the task.

Materials:

- folder with pockets
- envelopes
- marking pens and pencils
- scissors
- stapler
- two-sided tape

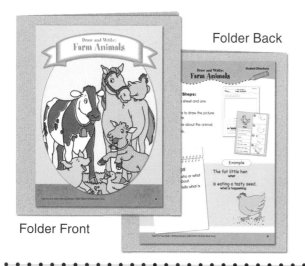

Folder Front

Folder Back

Steps to Follow:

1. Laminate the cover. Tape it to the front of the folder.

2. Laminate the student directions page. Tape it to the back of the folder.

3. Place activity sheets, writing paper, and any other supplies in the left-hand pocket.

4. Laminate the task cards. Place each set of task cards in an envelope. Place the labeled envelopes in the right-hand pocket.

5. If needed for the center, laminate the sorting mat and place it in the right-hand pocket of the folder.

6. If needed for the center, laminate and assemble the self-checking answer key pages into a booklet. Place them in the left-hand pocket of the folder.

Student Portfolio

If desired, make a writing portfolio for each student. Reproduce pages 5 and 6 for each student. Attach the cover to the front of a file folder. Attach the student center checklist to the inside front cover of the folder. Place the portfolio folders in an area accessible to both students and teacher.

Center Checklist

Student Names

Centers

Centers													
Draw and Write: Farm Animals													
All About Me													
Tool Time													
Make a Sentence													
Five on a List													
Write a Rhyme													
Let's Cook													
Story Puzzles													
Ask Gabby													
Favorite Things													
Write a Letter													
Write It Right!													
Pick a Story													

My Writing Portfolio

_____

Name

Writing Centers Checklist

Name _____

Check the writing centers that you have completed.

- ❏ Draw and Write: Farm Animals
- ❏ All About Me
- ❏ Tool Time
- ❏ Make a Sentence
- ❏ Five on a List
- ❏ Write a Rhyme
- ❏ Let's Cook

- ❏ Story Puzzles
- ❏ Ask Gabby
- ❏ Favorite Things
- ❏ Write a Letter
- ❏ Write It Right!
- ❏ Pick a Story

Draw and Write:
Farm Animals

Task Cards

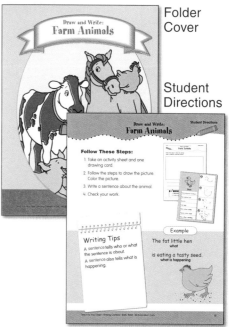

Folder Cover

Student Directions

Preparing the Center

1. Prepare a folder following the directions on page 3.

   Cover—page 9

   Student Directions—page 11

   Task Cards—pages 13–23

2. Reproduce a supply of the activity sheet on page 8.

Using the Center

1. The student selects a task card and an activity sheet.

2. The student follows the drawing steps to draw the picture described on the card. The student is encouraged to color the completed picture.

3. Next, the student uses the word bank on the card to write a sentence below the final picture. How to write a complete sentence is modeled in the student directions.

4. Finally, the student evaluates the writing task using the checklist on the activity sheet.

Name _____

Draw and Write:
Farm Animals

Follow the steps to draw the animal.
Write a sentence about the animal.

_____

_____

_____

✓ Check Your Work

- ○ I followed the directions to make a picture.
- ○ I wrote a sentence about the picture.

Draw and Write:
Farm Animals

10

Follow These Steps:

1. Take an activity sheet and one drawing card.

2. Follow the steps to draw the picture. Color the picture.

3. Write a sentence about the animal.

4. Check your work.

Writing Tips

A sentence tells who or what the sentence is about.

A sentence also tells what is happening.

Example

The fat little hen
what

is eating a tasty seed.
what is happening

Chicken

Has feathers
Has claws
Clucks
Lays eggs
Male called a **rooster**
Female called a **hen**
Baby called a **chick**

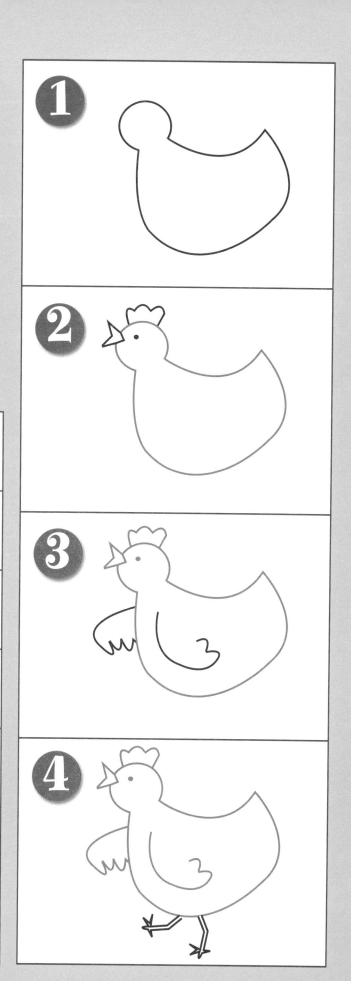

Draw and Write:
Farm Animals

© Evan-Moor Corp. • EMC 6002

Pig

Has short, stiff hair
Nose is called a snout
Little tail is curled
Snorts
Male called a **boar**
Female called a **sow**
Baby called a **piglet**

Draw and Write:
Farm Animals

© Evan-Moor Corp. • EMC 6002

Goat

Has fur
Has hoofs and short horns
Bleats
Has little beard under chin
Male called a **billy**
Female called a **nanny**
Baby called a **kid**

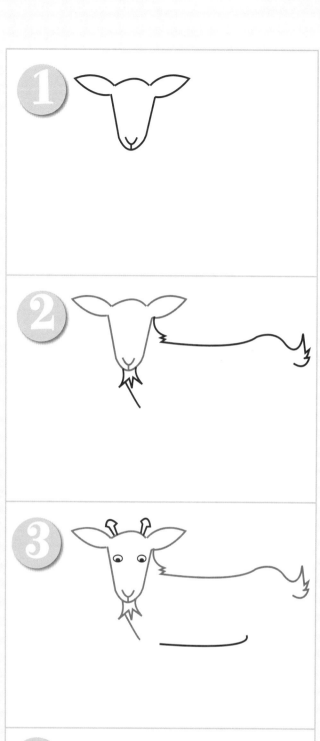

Draw and Write:
Farm Animals

© Evan-Moor Corp. • EMC 6002

Cow

Has short hair
Has hoofs
Has a long tail
Moos
Male called a **bull**
Female called a **cow**
Baby called a **calf**

Draw and Write:
Farm Animals

© Evan-Moor Corp. • EMC 6002

Horse

Has thick hair
Has hoofs
Has a mane and a long tail
Neighs
Male called a **stallion**
Female called a **mare**
Baby called a **foal**

Draw and Write:
Farm Animals

© Evan-Moor Corp. • EMC 6002

Duck

Has waterproof feathers
Has webbed feet
Quacks
Lays eggs
Male called a **drake**
Female called a **duck**
Baby called a **duckling**

Draw and Write:
Farm Animals

© Evan-Moor Corp. • EMC 6002

All About Me

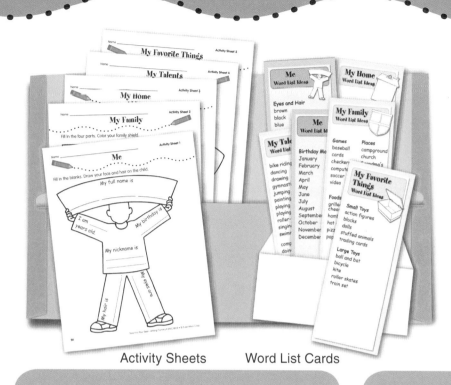

Activity Sheets   Word List Cards

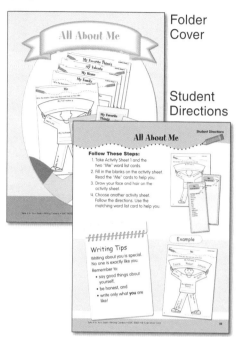

Folder Cover

Student Directions

Preparing the Center

1. Prepare a folder following the directions on page 3.

    Cover—page 31

    Student Directions—page 33

    Word List Cards—pages 35–39

2. Reproduce a supply of the activity sheets on pages 26–30.

Using the Center

1. The student selects the "Me" activity sheet on page 26 and the corresponding word list card on page 35.

2. The student completes the activity sheet. The student uses the word list card to help with ideas and spelling. The student also draws his/her face on the outline of the child. How to write correct personal information is modeled in the student directions.

3. The student chooses another activity sheet and matching word list card to complete.

    Note: The teacher may choose to have the student complete all five activity sheets for an "All About Me" booklet.

Name _____

Me

Fill in the blanks. Draw your face and hair on the child.

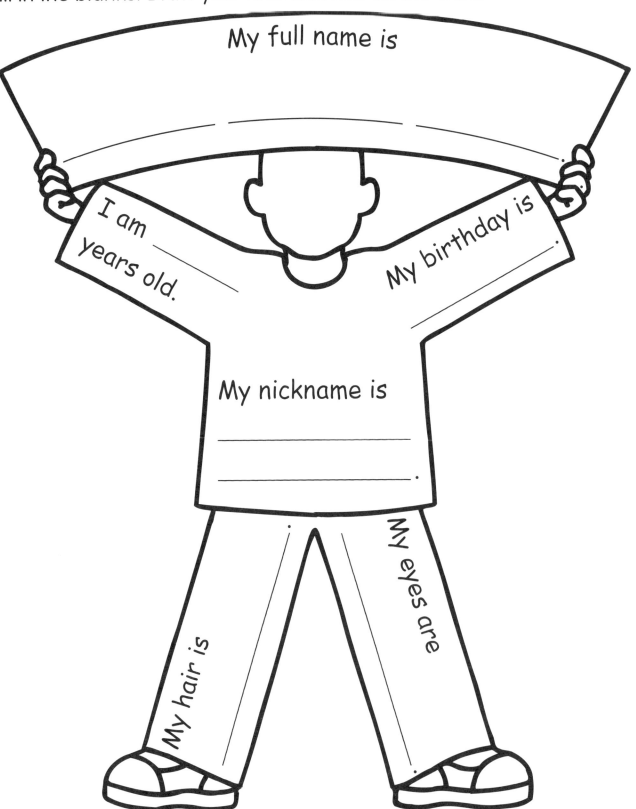

My full name *is*

I am _____ years old.

My birthday is

My nickname is

My hair is

My eyes are

 Take It to Your Seat—Writing Centers • EMC 6002 • © Evan-Moor Corp.

Name _____

My Family

Fill in the four parts. Color your family shield.

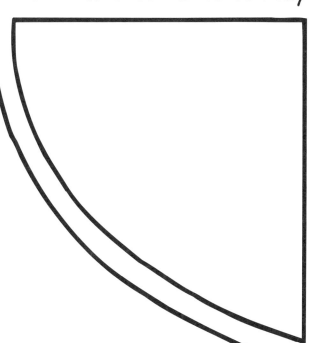

1. Names of Family Members

2. Places We Like to Visit

3. Games We Like to Play

4. Foods We Like to Eat

Name _____

My Home

Fill in the blanks. Color the house.

I live in a/an

_____ .

My address is:

_____

street/apt. number

_____

city

_____

state

_____

zip code

Take It to Your Seat—Writing Centers • EMC 6002 • © Evan-Moor Corp.

Name _____

My Talents

Write five things you are good at doing. Color the star.

My Favorite Things

Fill in the blanks. Color the toy box.

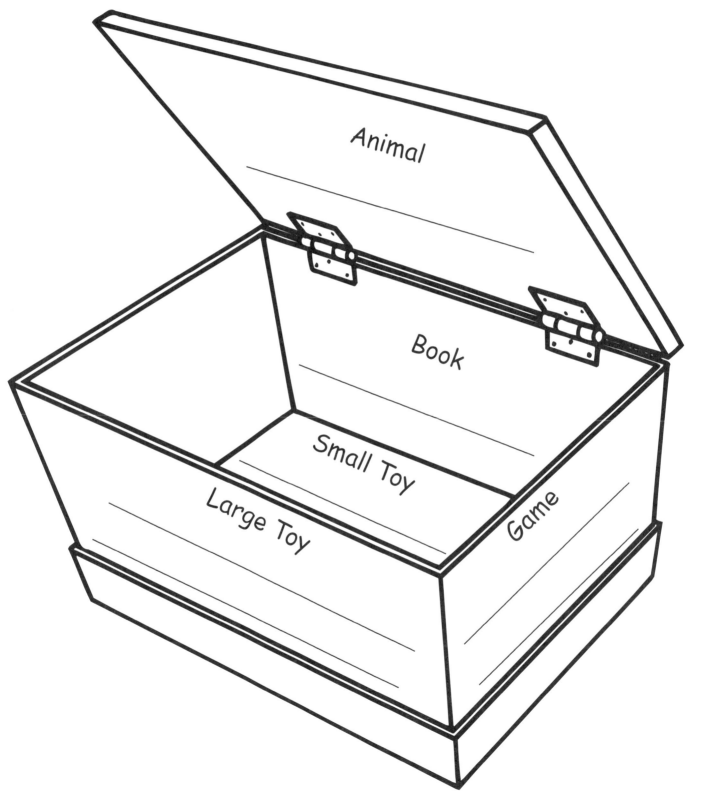

Animal

Book

Small Toy

Large Toy

Game

All About Me

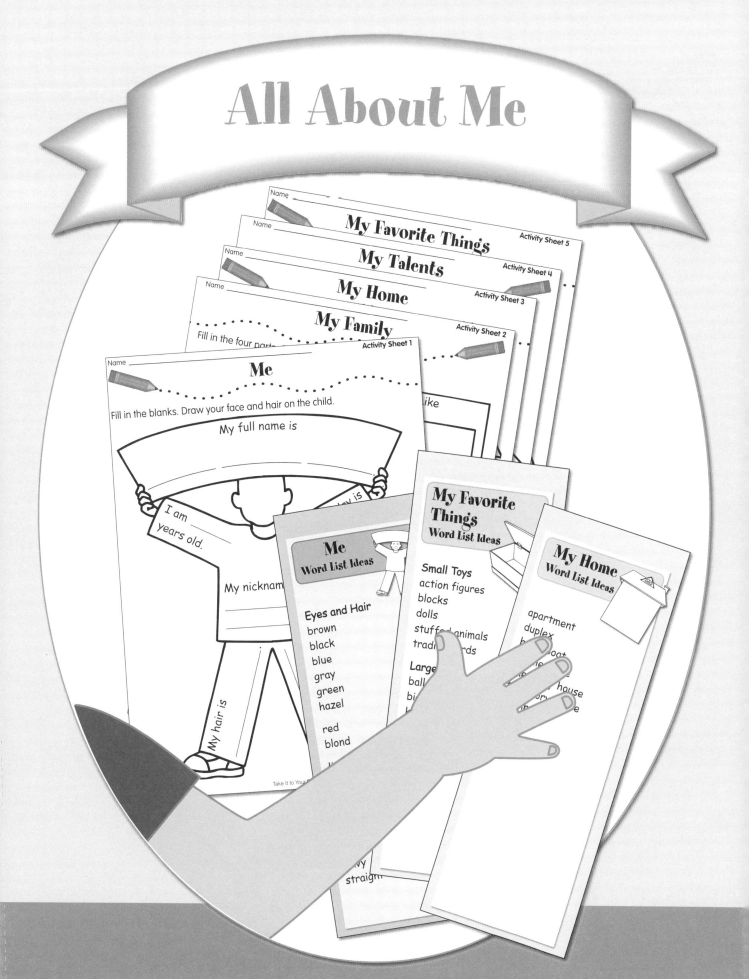

Name _____
My Favorite Things
Activity Sheet 5

Name _____
My Talents
Activity Sheet 4

Name _____
My Home
Activity Sheet 3

My Family
Activity Sheet 2
Fill in the four parts...

Name _____
Activity Sheet 1
Me
Fill in the blanks. Draw your face and hair on the child.

My full name is

I am _____ years old.

My nickname

My hair is

Me
Word List Ideas

Eyes and Hair
brown
black
blue
gray
green
hazel

red
blond

wavy
straight

My Favorite Things
Word List Ideas

Small Toys
action figures
blocks
dolls
stuffed animals
trading cards

Large
ball
bi...

My Home
Word List Ideas

apartment
duplex
...boat
...house

32

Take It to Your Seat—Writing Centers • EMC 6002 • © Evan-Moor Corp.

All About Me

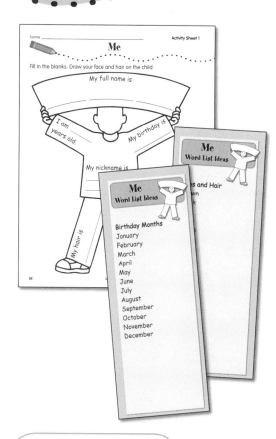

Follow These Steps:

1. Take Activity Sheet 1 and the two "Me" word list cards.

2. Fill in the blanks on the activity sheet. Read the "Me" cards to help you.

3. Draw your face and hair on the activity sheet.

4. Choose another activity sheet. Follow the directions. Use the matching word list card to help you.

Writing Tips

Writing about you is special. No one is exactly like you.

Remember to:

- say good things about yourself,
- be honest, and
- write only what **you** are like!

Example

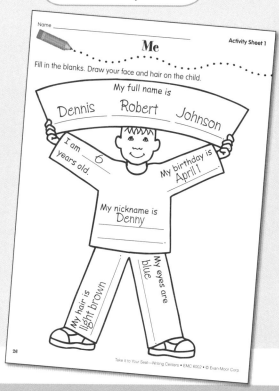

34

Me
Word List Ideas

Birthday Months

January

February

March

April

May

June

July

August

September

October

November

December

Me
Word List Ideas

Eyes and Hair

brown

black

blue

gray

green

hazel

red

blond

light

medium

dark

short

long

curly

wavy

straight

All About Me

© Evan-Moor Corp. • EMC 6002

All About Me

© Evan-Moor Corp. • EMC 6002

My Family
Word List Ideas

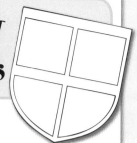

Games

baseball

cards

checkers

computer

soccer

video

Foods

grilled cheese

hamburger

hot dog

pizza

popcorn

Places

campground

church

Grandma's house

library

museum

park

playground

zoo

desert

forest

lake

mountains

river

My Home
Word List Ideas

apartment

duplex

houseboat

mobile home

one-story house

two-story house

townhouse

All About Me

All About Me

© Evan-Moor Corp. • EMC 6002

My Talents
Word List Ideas

bike riding

dancing

drawing

gymnastics

jumping rope

painting

playing piano

playing sports

roller-skating

singing

swimming

computer

doing puzzles

journal writing

math facts

reading

spelling

My Favorite Things
Word List Ideas

Small Toys

action figures

blocks

dolls

stuffed animals

trading cards

Large Toys

ball and bat

bicycle

kite

roller skates

train set

All About Me

All About Me

© Evan-Moor Corp. • EMC 6002

Tool Time

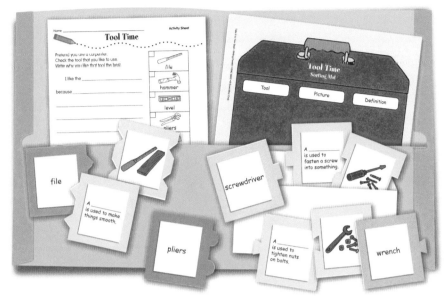

Puzzle Pieces

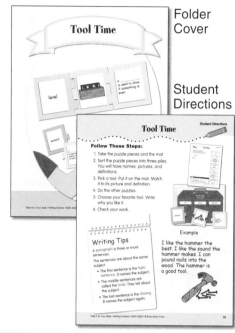

Folder Cover

Student Directions

Preparing the Center

1. Prepare a folder following the directions on page 3.

    Cover—page 43

    Student Directions—page 45

    Sorting Mat—page 47

    Puzzle Pieces—pages 49–55

2. Reproduce a supply of the activity sheet on page 42.

Using the Center

1. First, the student sorts the puzzle pieces into three piles—names, pictures, and definitions—on the sorting mat.

2. Next, the student reads and matches three cards at a time to complete a puzzle.

3. The student repeats the steps to complete the other seven puzzles.

4. Then the student chooses his or her favorite tool. The student writes a paragraph telling why that tool is the best. How to write a paragraph is modeled in the student directions.

5. Finally, the student evaluates the writing task using the checklist on the activity sheet.

Name _____

Tool Time

Pretend you are a carpenter.
Check the tool that you like to use.
Write why you like that tool the best.

    I like the _____

because _____

_____

_____

_____

_____

_____

☐	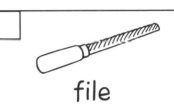 file
☐	 hammer
☐	 level
☐	 pliers
☐	 saw
☐	 screwdriver
☐	 tape measure
☐	 wrench

✔ **Check Your Work**

◯ I chose a tool.

◯ I wrote a paragraph about the tool.

◯ I gave reasons why I like the tool the best.

Tool Time

level

A _____ is used to show if something is even.

wrench

A _____ is used to tighten nuts on bolts.

pliers

_____ are used to hold things in place.

Tool Time

Follow These Steps:

1. Take the puzzle pieces and the mat.

2. Sort the puzzle pieces into three piles. You will have names, pictures, and definitions.

3. Pick a tool. Put it on the mat. Match it to its picture and definition.

4. Do the other puzzles.

5. Choose your favorite tool. Write why you like it.

6. Check your work.

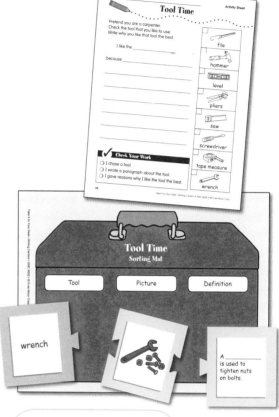

Example

Writing Tips

A paragraph is three or more sentences.

The sentences are about the same subject.

- The first sentence is the topic sentence. It names the subject.
- The middle sentences are called the body. They tell about the subject.
- The last sentence is the closing. It names the subject again.

I like the hammer the best. I like the sound the hammer makes. I can pound nails into the wood. The hammer is a good tool.

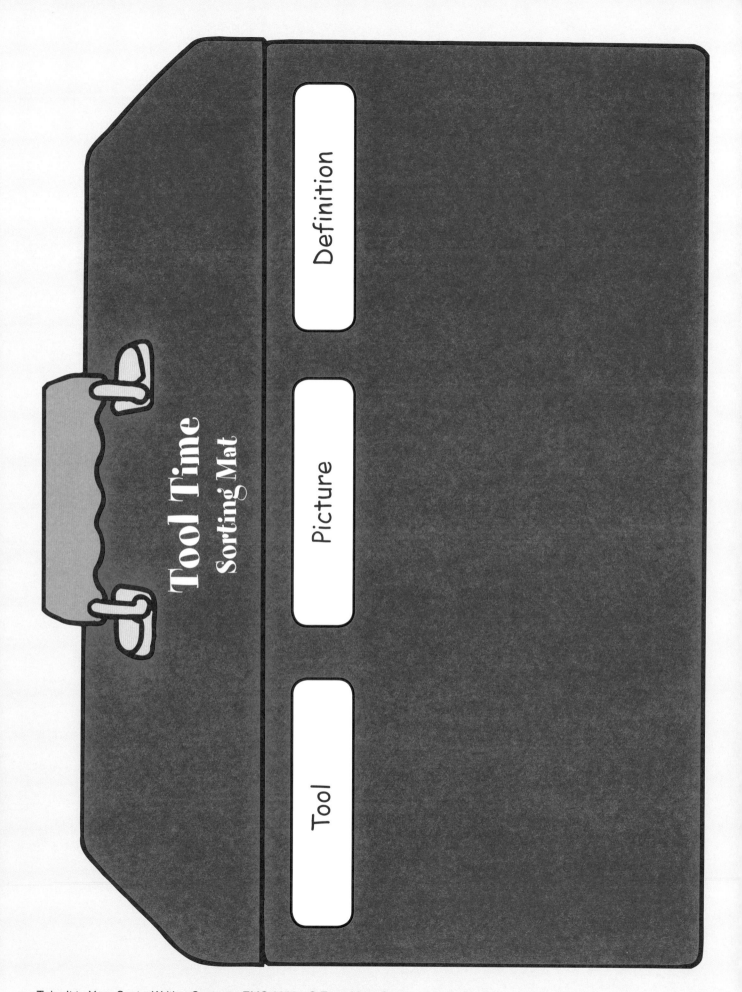

Tool Time
Sorting Mat

Definition

Picture

Tool

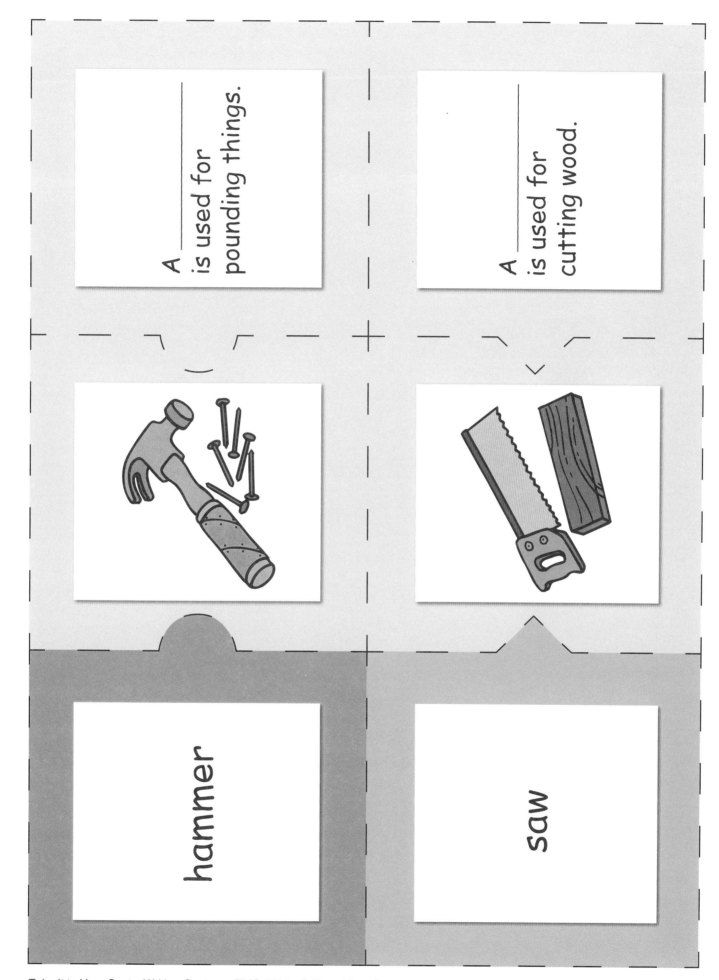

A _____
is used for
pounding things.

A _____
is used for
cutting wood.

hammer

saw

Tool Time

© Evan-Moor Corp. • EMC 6002

Tool Time

© Evan-Moor Corp. • EMC 6002

Tool Time

© Evan-Moor Corp. • EMC 6002

Tool Time

© Evan-Moor Corp. • EMC 6002

Tool Time

© Evan-Moor Corp. • EMC 6002

Tool Time

© Evan-Moor Corp. • EMC 6002

A _____ is used to fasten a screw into something.

A _____ is used to tighten nuts on bolts.

screwdriver

wrench

Tool Time

© Evan-Moor Corp. • EMC 6002

Tool Time

© Evan-Moor Corp. • EMC 6002

Tool Time

© Evan-Moor Corp. • EMC 6002

Tool Time

© Evan-Moor Corp. • EMC 6002

Tool Time

© Evan-Moor Corp. • EMC 6002

Tool Time

© Evan-Moor Corp. • EMC 6002

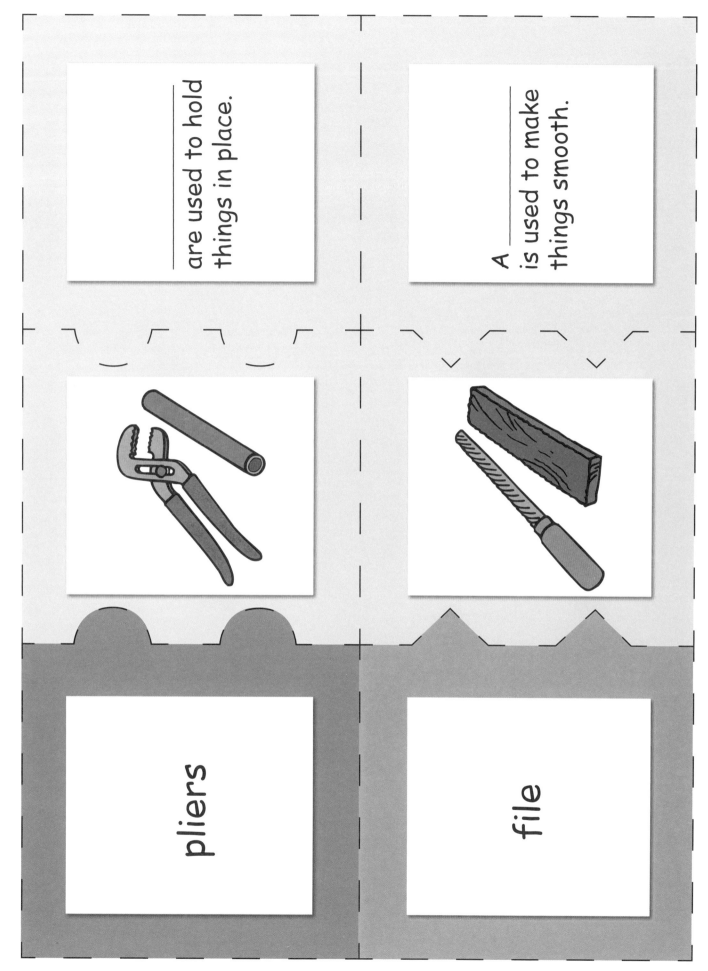

_____ are used to hold things in place.

A _____ is used to make things smooth.

pliers

file

Tool Time

© Evan-Moor Corp. • EMC 6002

Tool Time

© Evan-Moor Corp. • EMC 6002

Tool Time

© Evan-Moor Corp. • EMC 6002

Tool Time

© Evan-Moor Corp. • EMC 6002

Tool Time

© Evan-Moor Corp. • EMC 6002

Tool Time

© Evan-Moor Corp. • EMC 6002

A _____ is used to show if something is even.

A _____ is used to measure the length of something.

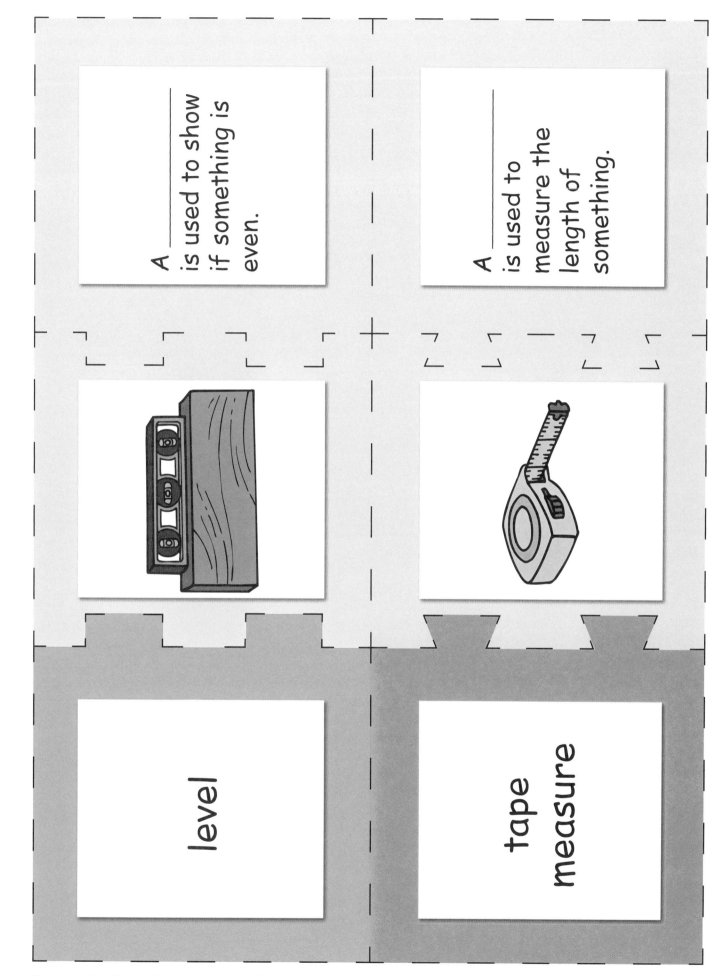

level

tape measure

Tool Time

Tool Time

Tool Time

Tool Time

Tool Time

Tool Time

Make a Sentence

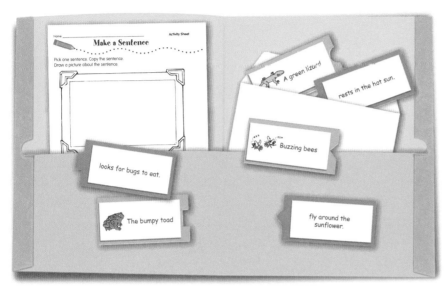

Puzzle Pieces

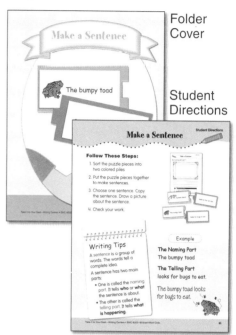

Folder Cover

Student Directions

Preparing the Center

1. Prepare a folder following the directions on page 3.

    Cover—page 59

    Student Directions—page 61

    Puzzle Pieces—pages 63–69

2. Reproduce a supply of the activity sheet on page 58.

Using the Center

1. The student takes the puzzle pieces and an activity sheet.

2. Next, the student puts the puzzles together to make complete sentences.

3. Then the student selects one sentence to copy and illustrate on the activity sheet. How to write a complete sentence is modeled in the student directions.

4. Finally, the student evaluates the writing task using the checklist on the activity sheet.

Name _____

Make a Sentence

Pick one sentence. Copy the sentence.
Draw a picture about the sentence.

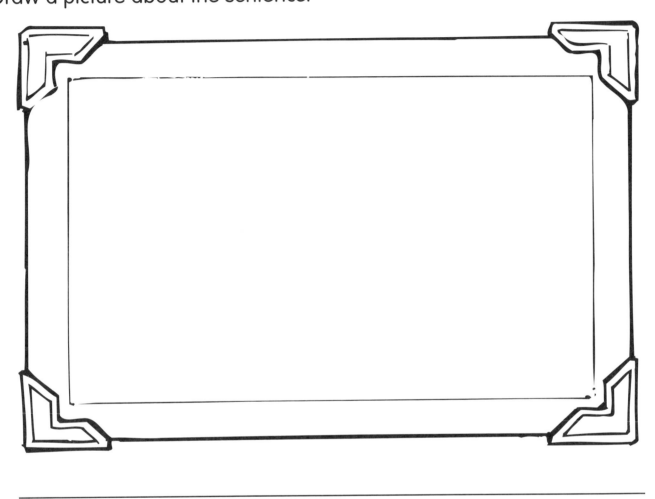

_____

_____

_____

_____

 Check Your Work

    ◯ I copied one sentence correctly.

    ◯ I drew a picture about the sentence.

Make a Sentence

 The bumpy toad

looks for bugs to eat

Make a Sentence

Follow These Steps:

1. Sort the puzzle pieces into two colored piles.

2. Put the puzzle pieces together to make sentences.

3. Choose one sentence. Copy the sentence. Draw a picture about the sentence.

4. Check your work.

Writing Tips

A sentence is a group of words. The words tell a complete idea.

A sentence has two main parts:

- One is called the naming part. It tells **who** or **what** the sentence is about.

- The other is called the telling part. It tells **what is happening**.

Example

The Naming Part
The bumpy toad

The Telling Part
looks for bugs to eat.

The bumpy toad looks for bugs to eat.

hops in the garden.

chews on a big bone.

sleeps on my bed.

The fluffy rabbit

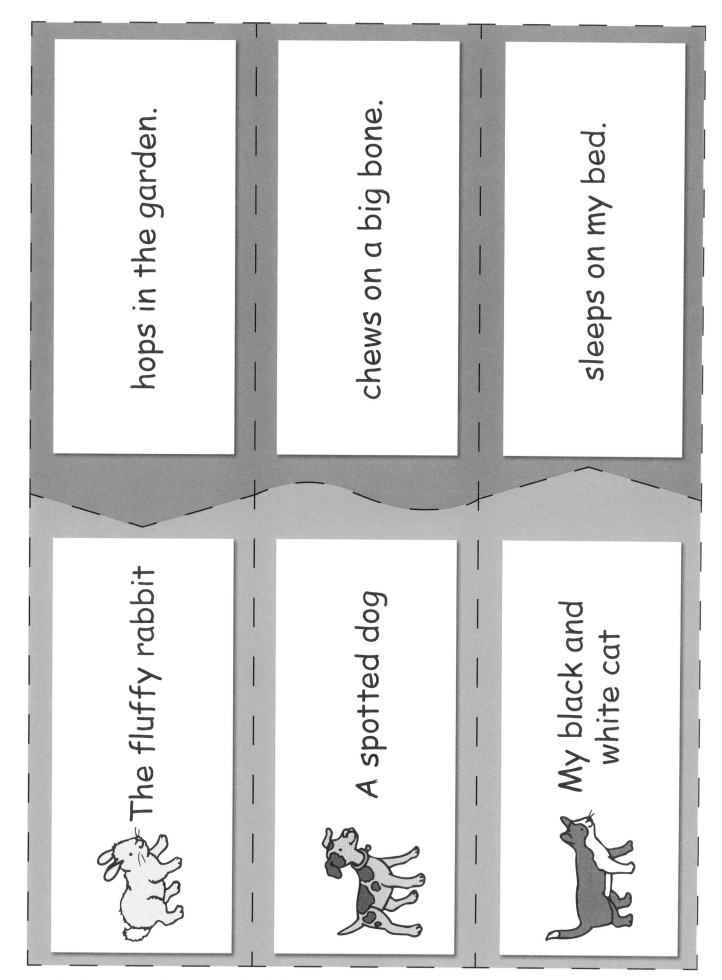

A spotted dog

My black and white cat

Make a Sentence

© Evan-Moor Corp. • EMC 6002

Make a Sentence

© Evan-Moor Corp. • EMC 6002

Make a Sentence

© Evan-Moor Corp. • EMC 6002

Make a Sentence

© Evan-Moor Corp. • EMC 6002

Make a Sentence

© Evan-Moor Corp. • EMC 6002

Make a Sentence

© Evan-Moor Corp. • EMC 6002

rests in the hot sun.

looks for bugs to eat.

fly around the sunflower.

A green lizard

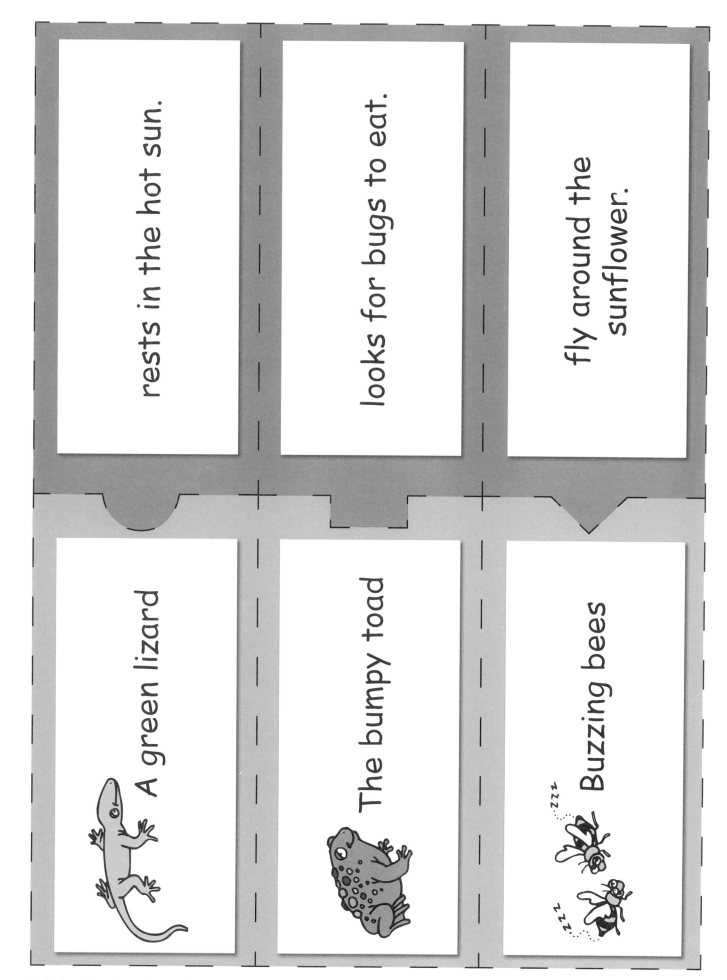

The bumpy toad

Buzzing bees

Make a Sentence

© Evan-Moor Corp. • EMC 6002

Make a Sentence

© Evan-Moor Corp. • EMC 6002

Make a Sentence

© Evan-Moor Corp. • EMC 6002

Make a Sentence

© Evan-Moor Corp. • EMC 6002

Make a Sentence

© Evan-Moor Corp. • EMC 6002

Make a Sentence

© Evan-Moor Corp. • EMC 6002

sits on the
bird feeder.

munch on
a green leaf.

swims in the ocean.

A yellow bird

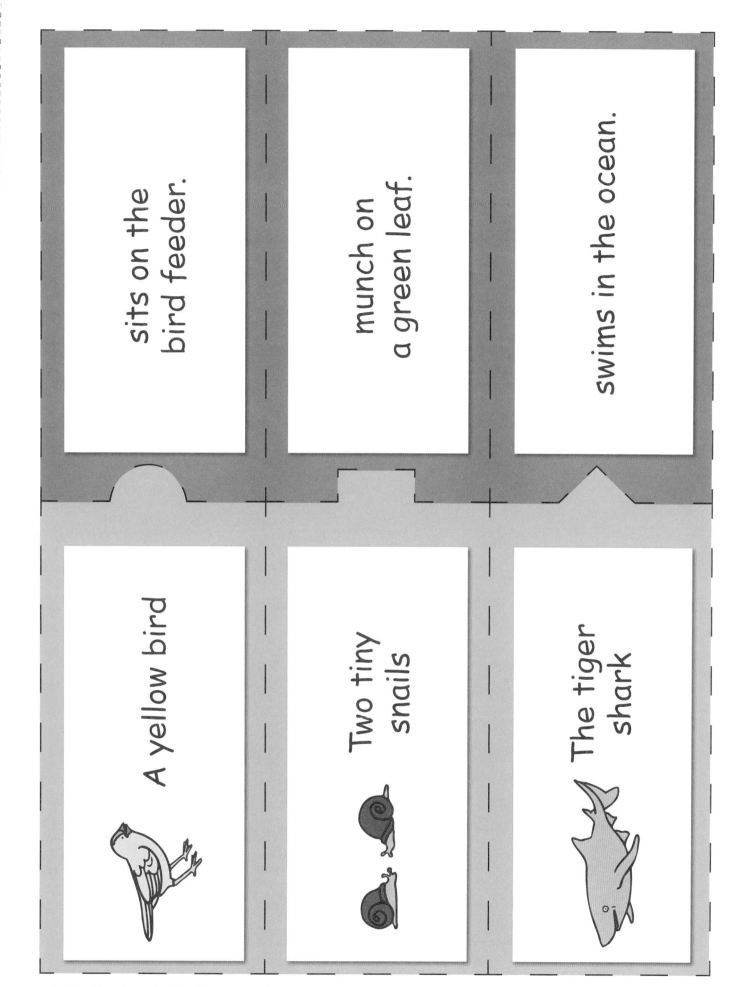

Two tiny
snails

The tiger
shark

Make a Sentence

© Evan-Moor Corp. • EMC 6002

Make a Sentence

© Evan-Moor Corp. • EMC 6002

Make a Sentence

© Evan-Moor Corp. • EMC 6002

Make a Sentence

© Evan-Moor Corp. • EMC 6002

Make a Sentence

© Evan-Moor Corp. • EMC 6002

Make a Sentence

© Evan-Moor Corp. • EMC 6002

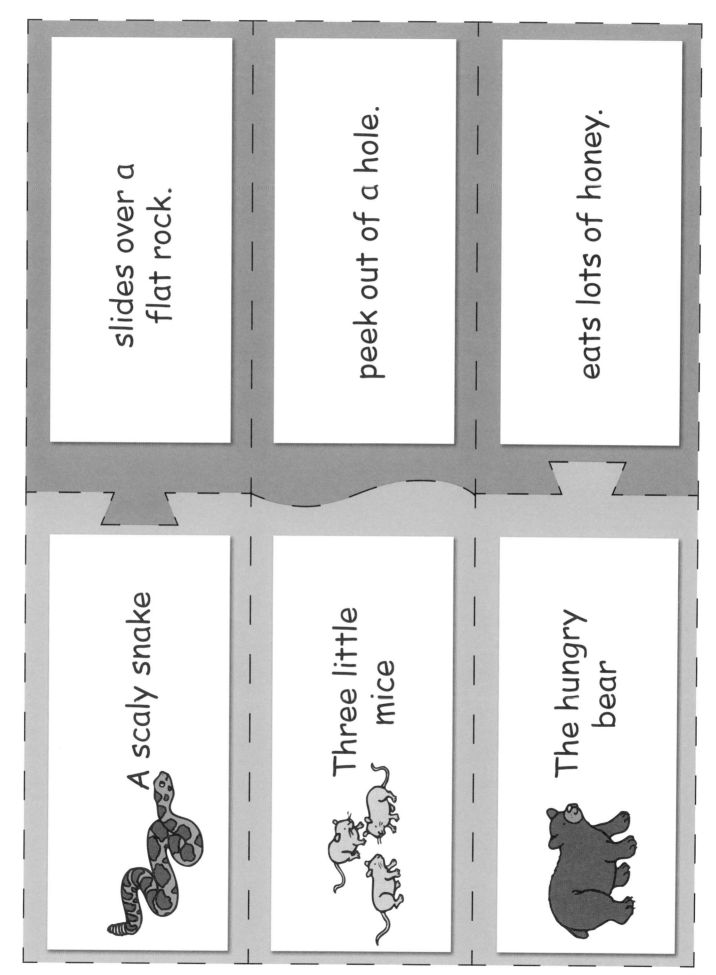

slides over a flat rock.

peek out of a hole.

eats lots of honey.

A scaly snake

Three little mice

The hungry bear

Make a Sentence

Make a Sentence

Make a Sentence

Make a Sentence

Make a Sentence

Make a Sentence

Five on a List

Task Cards

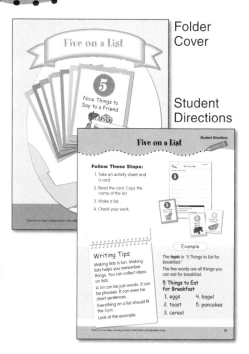

Folder Cover

Student Directions

Preparing the Center

1. Prepare a folder following the directions on page 3.

   Cover—page 73

   Student Directions—page 75

   Task Cards—pages 77–81

2. Reproduce a supply of the activity sheet on page 72.

Using the Center

1. The student selects a task card and an activity sheet.

2. Next, the student copies the title of the card onto the activity sheet.

3. Then the student writes a list of five things that fit the category. How to write a list is modeled in the student directions.

4. Finally, the student evaluates the writing task using the checklist on the activity sheet.

Name _____

Five on a List

Name the list. Write 5 things.

 _____

1. _____

2. _____

3. _____

4. _____

5. _____

 Check Your Work

◯ I wrote the name of the list.
◯ I wrote five things.
◯ The five things are all about the topic.

Five on a List

5

Nice Things to
Say to a Friend

Name

Five on a List

Activity Sheet

Name the list. Write 5 things.

5 Nice Things to Say to a Friend

1. Thank you.

2. Come play with m

3.

4.

...e name of the list.
...te five things.
...e five things are all about the topic.

Take It to Your Seat—Writing Centers • EMC 6002 • © Evan-Moor Corp.

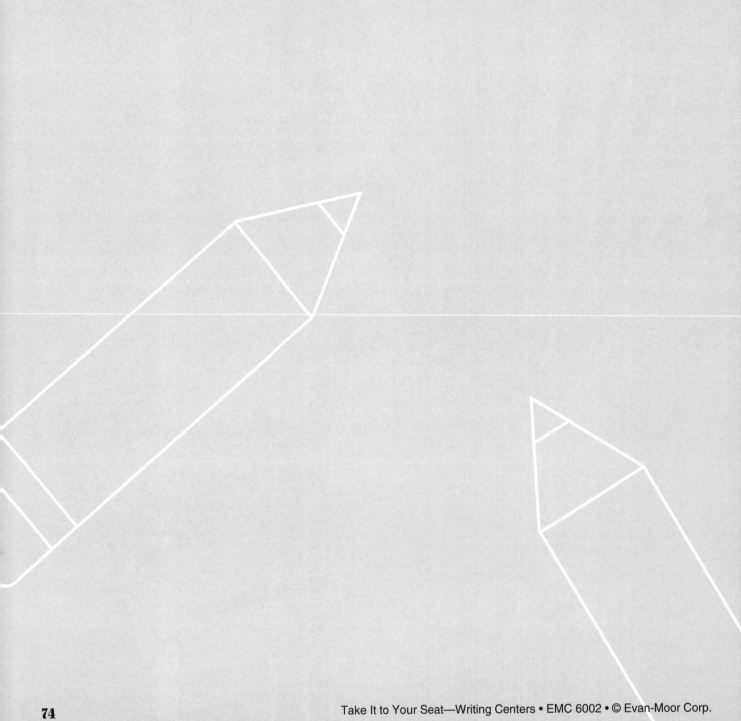

Five on a List

Follow These Steps:

1. Take an activity sheet and a card.

2. Read the card. Copy the name of the list.

3. Make a list.

4. Check your work.

Writing Tips

Making lists is fun. Making lists helps you remember things. You can collect ideas on lists.

A list can be just words. It can be phrases. It can even be short sentences.

Everything on a list should fit the topic.

Look at the example.

Example

The **topic** is "5 Things to Eat for Breakfast."

The five words are all things you can eat for breakfast.

5 Things to Eat for Breakfast

1. eggs
2. toast
3. cereal
4. bagel
5. pancakes

76

5
Good Things About a Pet

5
Things I Need at School

5
Things to Eat at a Picnic

5
Toys with Wheels

Five on a List

Five on a List

Five on a List

Five on a List

5

Things That
Can Fly

5

Cold Things at the
Grocery Store

5

Things That
Are Sweet

5

Things to Do
at the Park

Five on a List

Five on a List

Five on a List

Five on a List

5

Things That
Are Round

5

Nice Things to
Say to a Friend

5

Things That
Are Smaller
Than My Hand

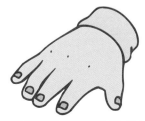

5

Things That
Are Bigger
Than a Car

Five on a List

Five on a List

Five on a List

Five on a List

Write a Rhyme

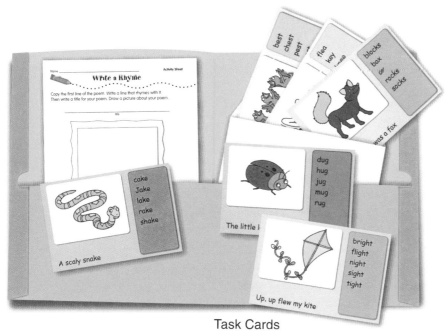

Task Cards

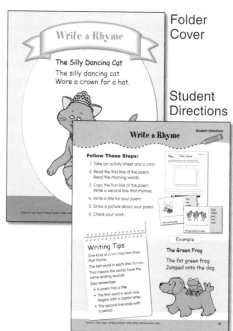

Folder Cover

Student Directions

Preparing the Center

1. Prepare a folder following the directions on page 3.

    Cover—page 85

    Student Directions—page 87

    Task Cards—pages 89–99

2. Reproduce a supply of the activity sheet on page 84.

Using the Center

1. The student selects one task card and an activity sheet.

2. Next, the student reads the line of a verse and the word list on the card. The student copies the line onto the activity sheet and writes a second line to complete a couplet. How to write a rhyming poem is modeled in the student directions.

3. The student writes a title for the poem.

4. Then the student draws a picture to illustrate the rhyme.

5. Finally, the student evaluates the writing task using the checklist on the activity sheet.

Write a Rhyme

Copy the first line of the poem. Write a line that rhymes with it.
Then write a title for your poem. Draw a picture about your poem.

_____
title

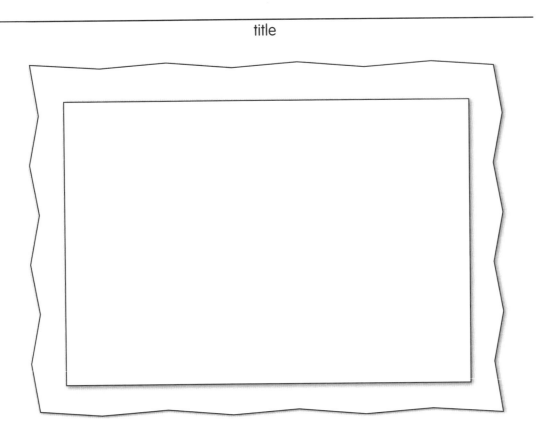

_____

_____

_____

✓ Check Your Work

○ My poem rhymes.
○ I wrote a good title.
○ My picture matches my poem.

Write a Couplets

The Silly Dancing Cat

The silly dancing cat
Wore a crown for a hat.

86

Write a Rhyme

Follow These Steps:

1. Take an activity sheet and a card.

2. Read the first line of the poem. Read the rhyming words.

3. Copy the first line of the poem. Write a second line that rhymes.

4. Write a title for your poem.

5. Draw a picture about your poem.

6. Check your work.

Writing Tips

One kind of poem has two lines that rhyme.

The last word in each line rhymes.

That means the words have the same ending sounds.

Also remember:

- A poem has a title.
- The first word in each line begins with a capital letter.
- The second line ends with a period.

Example

The Green Frog

The fat green frog
Jumped onto the dog.

88

dog
fog
hog
jog
log

The fat green frog

bat
hat
mat
rat
splat

The silly black cat

Write a Rhyme

© Evan-Moor Corp. • EMC 6002

Write a Rhyme

© Evan-Moor Corp. • EMC 6002

flea
key
knee
me
tree

The buzzing bee

best
chest
pest
rest
west

Three birds in a nest

Write a Rhyme

Write a Rhyme

© Evan-Moor Corp. • EMC 6002

blocks

box

ox

rocks

socks

There once was a fox

dug

hug

jug

mug

rug

The little ladybug

Write a Rhyme

Write a Rhyme

boat
coat
float
note
throat

The billy goat

bay
clay
play
stay
tray

One summer day

Write a Rhyme

Write a Rhyme

cake
Jake
lake
rake
shake

A scaly snake

bright
flight
night
sight
tight

Up, up flew my kite

Write a Rhyme

© Evan-Moor Corp. • EMC 6002

Write a Rhyme

© Evan-Moor Corp. • EMC 6002

day

play

stay

sway

yesterday

I found a sea star by the bay

brown

down

frown

gown

town

The happy clown

Write a Rhyme

© Evan-Moor Corp. • EMC 6002

Write a Rhyme

© Evan-Moor Corp. • EMC 6002

Let's Cook

Task Cards

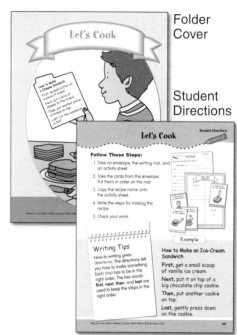

Folder Cover

Student Directions

Preparing the Center

1. Prepare a folder following the directions on page 3.

    Cover—page 103

    Student Directions—page 105

    Sorting Mat—page 107

    Recipe Cards—pages 109–115

2. Reproduce a supply of the activity sheet on page 102. Label and then place each set of recipe cards in a small envelope.

Using the Center

1. The student selects a recipe envelope, the sorting mat, and an activity sheet.

2. Next, the student places the four recipe cards in order on the sorting mat. The recipe cards are self-checking.

3. Then the student writes the recipe steps in order. A word bank is provided on the back of card 1 in each set. How to write steps is modeled in the student directions.

4. Finally, the student evaluates the writing task using the checklist on the activity sheet.

Let's Cook

Write the name of the recipe. Write the directions.

How to Make _____

First, _____

_____

Next, _____

_____

Then, _____

_____

Last, _____

_____

✔ Check Your Work

- ○ My directions make sense.
- ○ My steps are in order.

Let's Cook

How to Make a Cheese Sandwich

First, spread butter on a piece of bread.

Next, put a slice of cheese on the bread.

Then, put another piece of bread on top.

Last, cut the sandwich in half.

Let's Cook

Follow These Steps:

1. Take an envelope, the mat, and an activity sheet.

2. Take the cards from the envelope. Put them in order on the mat.

3. Copy the recipe name onto the activity sheet.

4. Write the steps for making the recipe.

5. Check your work.

Writing Tips

How-to writing gives directions. The directions tell you how to make something. Each step has to be in the right order. The key words **first**, **next**, **then**, and **last** are used to keep the steps in the right order.

Example

How to Make an Ice-Cream Sandwich

First, get a small scoop of vanilla ice cream.

Next, put it on top of a big chocolate chip cookie.

Then, put another cookie on top.

Last, gently press down on the cookie.

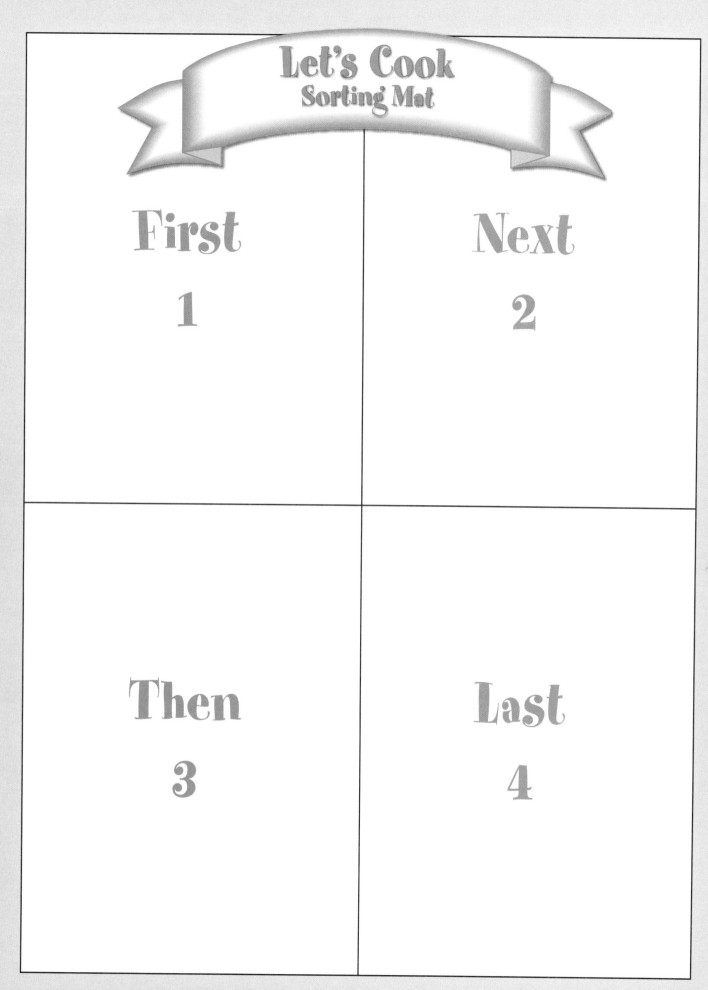

Let's Cook
Sorting Mat

First
1

Next
2

Then
3

Last
4

A Peanut Butter and Jelly Sandwich

A Peanut Butter and Jelly Sandwich

A Peanut Butter and Jelly Sandwich

A Peanut Butter and Jelly Sandwich

Word Bank

bread	sandwich
peanut butter	knife
jelly	spread
plate	cut

2
Let's Cook

1
Let's Cook

4
Let's Cook

3
Let's Cook

Chocolate Milk

Chocolate Milk

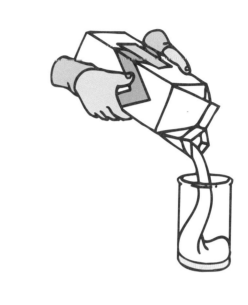

Chocolate Milk

Chocolate Milk

Word Bank

chocolate	spoon
syrup	pour
milk	stir
glass	

2

Let's Cook

1

Let's Cook

4

Let's Cook

3

Let's Cook

Vanilla Pudding

Vanilla Pudding

Vanilla Pudding

Vanilla Pudding

Word Bank

vanilla	measuring
pudding mix	cup
carton of milk	whisk
mixing bowl	one cup
small bowl	stir
spoon	

2
Let's Cook

1
Let's Cook

4
Let's Cook

3
Let's Cook

An Ice-Cream Sundae

An Ice-Cream Sundae

An Ice-Cream Sundae

An Ice-Cream Sundae

Word Bank

ice cream

chocolate syrup

whipped cream

cherry

bowl

scoop

squirt

spoon

2

Let's Cook

© Evan-Moor Corp. • EMC 6002

1

Let's Cook

© Evan-Moor Corp. • EMC 6002

4

Let's Cook

© Evan-Moor Corp. • EMC 6002

3

Let's Cook

© Evan-Moor Corp. • EMC 6002

Story Puzzles

Puzzle Pieces

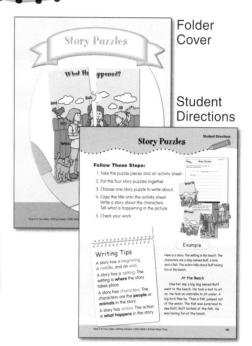

Folder Cover

Student Directions

Preparing the Center

1. Prepare a folder following the directions on page 3.

   Cover—page 119

   Student Directions—page 121

   Puzzle Pieces—pages 123–129

2. Reproduce a supply of the activity sheet on page 118.

Using the Center

1. The student takes the story puzzle pieces and an activity sheet.

2. Next, the student puts the four story puzzles together.

3. Then the student selects one of the completed puzzles. The student writes a story about the incident shown in the picture. How to write a story is modeled in the student directions.

4. Finally, the student evaluates the writing task using the checklist on the activity sheet.

Name _____

Story Puzzles

Pick one story puzzle. Copy the title of the story.
Write a story about the picture.

_____
Write the title here.

One day _____

_____

_____

_____

_____

_____

_____

✔ **Check Your Work**

◯ I copied the title.
◯ My story tells about the characters.
◯ My story tells about the setting.
◯ My story tells what is happening.

Story Puzzles

Story Puzzles

Follow These Steps:

1. Take the puzzle pieces and an activity sheet.

2. Put the four story puzzles together.

3. Choose one story puzzle to write about.

4. Copy the title onto the activity sheet.
   Write a story about the characters.
   Tell what is happening in the picture.

5. Check your work.

Writing Tips

A story has a beginning, a middle, and an end.

A story has a setting. The setting is **where** the story takes place.

A story has characters. The characters are the **people** or **animals** in the story.

A story has action. The action is **what happens** in the story.

Example

Here is a story. The setting is the beach. The characters are a dog named Ruff, a bird, and a fish. The action tells about Ruff having fun at the beach.

At the Beach

One hot day a big dog named Ruff went to the beach. He took a mat to sit on. He took an umbrella to sit under. A big bird flew by. Then a fish jumped out of the water. The fish was surprised to see Ruff. Ruff barked at the fish. He was having fun at the beach.

Stan and Goldie

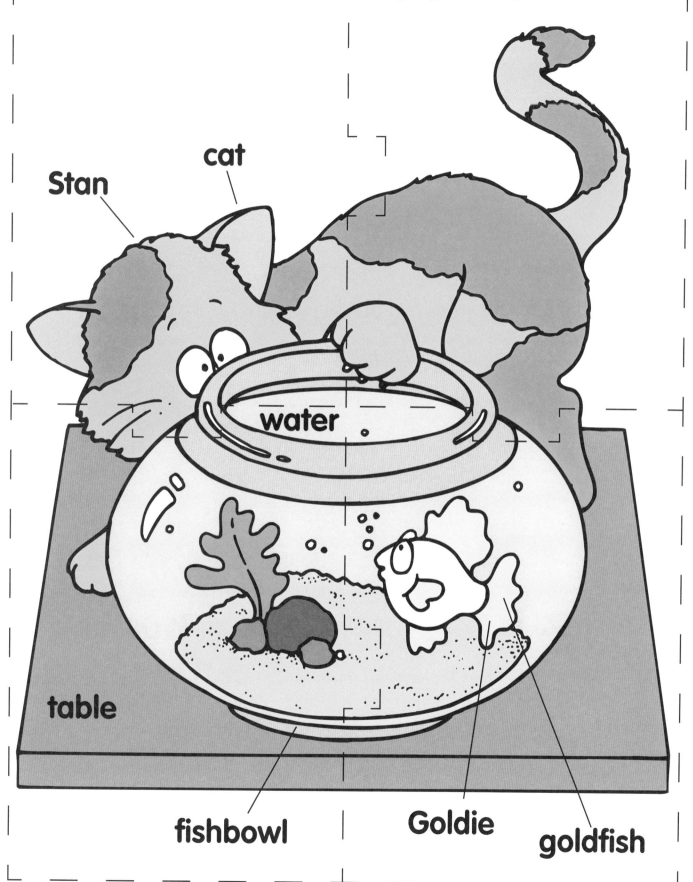

Stan

cat

water

table

fishbowl

Goldie

goldfish

Story Puzzles

Story Puzzles

Story Puzzles

Story Puzzles

At the Beach

sun

bird

umbrella

water fish

dog

lemonade

beach mat

ice cream

Story Puzzles

Story Puzzles

© Evan-Moor Corp. • EMC 6002

Story Puzzles

© Evan-Moor Corp. • EMC 6002

Story Puzzles

© Evan-Moor Corp. • EMC 6002

The Three Billy Goats Gruff

big goat

little goat

middle goat

bridge

troll

grass

Story Puzzles

Story Puzzles

Story Puzzles

Story Puzzles

What Happened?

Story Puzzles

© Evan-Moor Corp. • EMC 6002

Story Puzzles

© Evan-Moor Corp. • EMC 6002

Story Puzzles

© Evan-Moor Corp. • EMC 6002

Story Puzzles

© Evan-Moor Corp. • EMC 6002

Ask Gabby

Task Cards

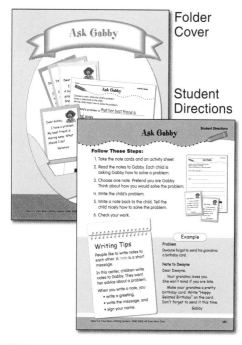

Folder Cover

Student Directions

Preparing the Center

1. Prepare a folder following the directions on page 3.

   Cover—page 133

   Student Directions—page 135

   Task Cards—pages 137–141

2. Reproduce a supply of the activity sheet on page 132.

Using the Center

1. The student takes the task cards and an activity sheet.

2. Next, the student reads the notes on the cards. The student chooses one of the notes to respond to as in an advice column.

3. Then the student writes the problem the child is facing. The student pretends to be "Dear Gabby" and writes a note back, giving advice on how to solve the child's problem. How to write a note is modeled in the student directions.

4. Finally, the student evaluates the writing task using the checklist on the activity sheet.

Ask Gabby

Choose a card. Write the child's problem.
Write a note back to the child.
Tell the child nicely how to solve the problem.

The child's problem is _____

_____ .

Dear _____ ,

_____

_____

_____

_____

Gabby

✓ Check Your Work

○ I wrote the problem.
○ I wrote a note back.
○ I gave good advice.

Ask Gabby

Dear Gabby,

I have a problem. My best friend is moving away. What should I do?

Veronica

Name _____

Ask Gabby

Activity Sheet

Choose a card. Write the child's problem. Write a note back to the child. Tell the child nicely how to solve the problem.

child's problem is that her best friend is

ng away .

eronica ,

s sad to see a friend move. Get her

dress. Ask girls in your class to help

letters to your friend. Then you

so lonely.

Ask Gabby

Follow These Steps:

1. Take the note cards and an activity sheet.

2. Read the notes to Gabby. Each child is asking Gabby how to solve a problem.

3. Choose one note. Pretend you are Gabby. Think about how you would solve the problem.

4. Write the child's problem.

5. Write a note back to the child. Tell the child nicely how to solve the problem.

6. Check your work.

Writing Tips

People like to write notes to each other. A note is a short message.

In this center, children write notes to Gabby. They want her advice about a problem.

When you write a note, you
- write a greeting,
- write the message, and
- sign your name.

Example

Problem

Dwayne forgot to send his grandma a birthday card.

Note to Dwayne

Dear Dwayne,

   Your grandma loves you. She won't mind if you are late.

   Make your grandma a pretty birthday card. Write "Happy Belated Birthday" on the card. Don't forget to send it this time.

                    Gabby

Dear Gabby,

    I have a problem. Jenny won't play with me at recess. What should I do?

    Samantha

Dear Gabby,

    I have a problem. My big brother won't help me with my homework. What should I do?

    Christopher

Dear Gabby,

    I have a problem. A big kid in fourth grade teases me. She calls me **Squirt**. What should I do?

    Tamara

Dear Gabby,

    I have a problem. I forgot to send my grandma a birthday card. What should I do?

    Dwayne

Ask Gabby

© Evan-Moor Corp. • EMC 6002

Ask Gabby

© Evan-Moor Corp. • EMC 6002

Ask Gabby

© Evan-Moor Corp. • EMC 6002

Ask Gabby

© Evan-Moor Corp. • EMC 6002

Dear Gabby,

I have a problem. My homework got all wet. What should I do?

Charlene

Dear Gabby,

I have a problem. I have to take out the garbage. I am too tired to do it every night. What should I do?

Beatrice

Dear Gabby,

I have a problem. My mom is having a baby. I feel jealous. What should I do?

Tyler

Dear Gabby,

I have a problem. My best friend is moving away. What should I do?

Veronica

Ask Gabby

Ask Gabby

Ask Gabby

Ask Gabby

Dear Gabby,

I have a problem. I forget to feed my dog every morning. What should I do?

Jackson

Dear Gabby,

I have a problem. I am always late for school. What should I do?

Jason

Dear Gabby,

I have a problem. I want a new pair of tennis shoes. My parents said, "No!" What should I do?

Hank

Dear Gabby,

I have a problem. My little sister keeps getting in my room. She messes things up. What should I do?

Lucy

Ask Gabby

Ask Gabby

Ask Gabby

Ask Gabby

Favorite Things

Task Cards

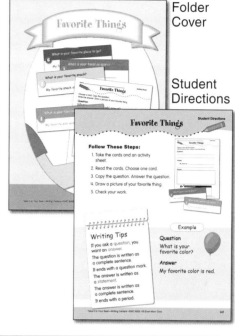

Folder Cover

Student Directions

Preparing the Center

1. Prepare a folder following the directions on page 3.

   Cover—page 145

   Student Directions—page 147

   Task Cards—pages 149 and 151

2. Reproduce a supply of the activity sheet on page 144.

Using the Center

1. The student takes the task cards and an activity sheet.

2. Next, the student reads the question and response starter cards. The student chooses his or her favorite card.

3. Then the student copies the question onto the activity sheet and writes a response. The student also draws a picture of the favorite thing. How to write a response to a question is modeled in the student directions.

4. Finally, the student evaluates the writing task using the checklist on the activity sheet.

Name _____

Favorite Things

Choose a card. Copy the question.
Write the answer. Draw a picture of your favorite thing.

Question

_____

_____

Answer

My favorite _____

_____ .

Picture

[ ]

✓ **Check Your Work**

○ I copied the question.
○ I answered the question.
○ I wrote complete sentences.
○ I drew my favorite thing.

Favorite Things

What is your favorite place to go?

6

My fa

What is your favorite sport?

5

What is your favorite snack?

3

My favorite snack

What is your favorite wild animal?

4

My favorite wild animal is _____.

Name _____

Favorite Things

Activity Sheet

Choose a card. Copy the question.
Write the answer. Draw a picture of your favorite thing.

Question

What is your fa___ wild animal?

_____ is a lion

Picture

___ences.
___rite thing.

Favorite Things

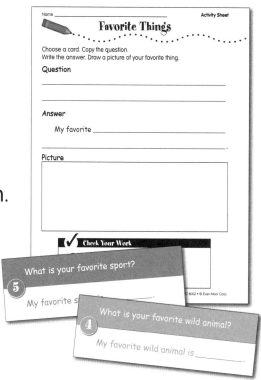

Follow These Steps:

1. Take the cards and an activity sheet.

2. Read the cards. Choose one card.

3. Copy the question. Answer the question.

4. Draw a picture of your favorite thing.

5. Check your work.

Writing Tips

If you ask a question, you want an answer.

The question is written as a complete sentence.

It ends with a question mark.

The answer is written as a statement.

The answer is written as a complete sentence.

It ends with a period.

Example

Question

What is your favorite color?

Answer

My favorite color is red.

What is your favorite color?

My favorite color is _____.

What is your favorite toy?

My favorite toy is _____.

What is your favorite snack?

My favorite snack is _____.

What is your favorite wild animal?

My favorite wild animal is _____.

Favorite Things

Favorite Things

Favorite Things

Favorite Things

5

What is your favorite sport?

My favorite sport is _____.

6

What is your favorite place to go?

My favorite place to go is _____.

7

What is your favorite kind of pet?

My favorite kind of pet is _____.

8

What is your favorite TV show?

My favorite TV show is _____.

Favorite Things

Favorite Things

Favorite Things

Favorite Things

Write a Letter

Task Cards

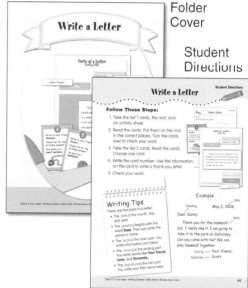

Folder Cover

Student Directions

Preparing the Center

1. Prepare a folder following the directions on page 3.

   Cover—page 155

   Student Directions—page 157

   Sorting Mat—page 159

   Task Cards—pages 161 and 163

      Set 1—Parts of a letter

      Set 2—Thank-you cards

2. Reproduce a supply of the activity sheet on page 154.

Using the Center

1. First, the student takes the parts of a letter cards, the sorting mat, and an activity sheet.

2. Next, the student places the parts of a letter in the correct places on the sorting mat. The cards are self-checking.

3. The student then takes and reads the four thank-you cards. The student chooses one card.

4. The student writes the number of the card on the activity sheet. Then the student writes a thank-you letter using the information on the card. How to write a letter is modeled in the student directions.

5. Finally, the student evaluates the writing task using the checklist on the activity sheet.

Name _____

Write a Letter

Card ☐

Write the thank-you letter.

_____
date

Dear _____ ,

_____

_____

_____

_____

_____

_____

✔ **Check Your Work**

○ I wrote today's date.
○ I wrote the friend's name in the greeting.
○ I wrote the body of the letter.
○ I wrote a closing.
○ I signed my name.

Write a Letter

Parts of a Letter
Sorting Mat

Date

November 15, 2006

Dear Angela,

Greeting

Thank you for the diary. Thank you for the purple pen, too. It even locks! I will keep the key in a safe place. I will write in my diary every day. I will lock it so my brother can't read it. Thank you again. You're the best!

Closing

Your best friend,

Signature

Carolina

1
Write to your friend **Shannon**.
Thank her for the birthday present.
She gave you a **heart necklace**.

2
Write to your friend **Jeremy**.
Thank him for the birthday present.
He gave you a **basketball**.

Write a Letter

Follow These Steps:

1. Take the Set 1 cards, the mat, and an activity sheet.

2. Read the cards. Put them on the mat in the correct places. Turn the cards over to check your work.

3. Take the Set 2 cards. Read the cards. Choose one card.

4. Write the card number. Use the information on the card to write a thank-you letter.

5. Check your work.

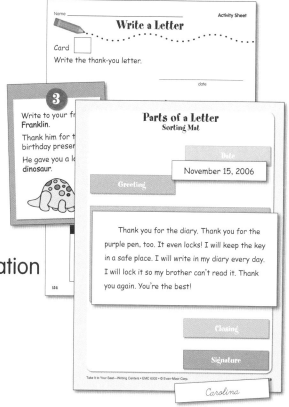

Writing Tips

There are five parts to a letter:

- The date is the month, day, and year.
- The greeting begins with the word **Dear**. Then you write the person's name.
- The body is the main part. You write information and ideas.
- The closing is the ending part. You write words like **Your friend,** **Love,** and **Sincerely,**.
- The signature is the last part. You write your first name here.

Example

Greeting   Date

May 2, 2006

Dear Sonny,

   Thank you for the baseball bat. I really like it. I am going to take it to the park on Saturday. Can you come with me? We can play baseball together.   Body

Closing —— Your friend,

Signature —— Scott

Parts of a Letter
Sorting Mat

Date

Greeting

Body

Closing

Signature

November 15, 2006

Dear Angela,

Your best friend,

Carolina

Thank you for the diary. Thank you for the purple pen, too. It even locks! I will keep the key in a safe place. I will write in my diary every day. I will lock it so my brother can't read it. Thank you again. You're the best!

Set 1   greeting

Write a Letter

Set 1   date

Write a Letter

Set 1   signature

Write a Letter

Set 1   closing

Write a Letter

Set 1   body

Write a Letter

1

Write to your friend **Shannon**.

Thank her for the birthday present.

She gave you a **heart necklace**.

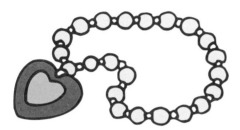

2

Write to your friend **Jeremy**.

Thank him for the birthday present.

He gave you a **basketball**.

3

Write to your friend **Franklin**.

Thank him for the birthday present.

He gave you a large **dinosaur**.

4

Write to your friend **Olivia**.

Thank her for the birthday present.

She gave you **two jump ropes**.

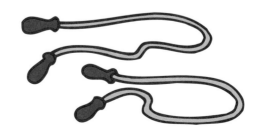

Set 2

Write a Letter

Set 2

Write a Letter

Set 2

Write a Letter

Set 2

Write a Letter

Write It Right!

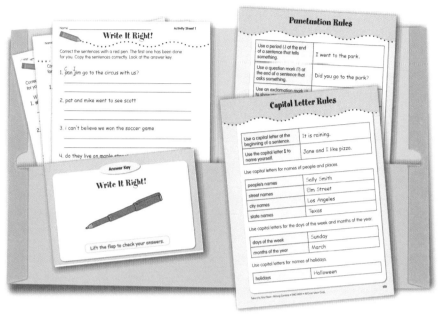

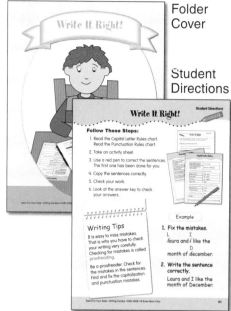

Folder Cover

Student Directions

Preparing the Center

1. Prepare a folder following the directions on page 3.

   Cover—page 169

   Student Directions—page 171

   Rule Charts—pages 173 and 175

   Answer Key—pages 177 and 178

2. Reproduce a supply of the activity sheets on pages 166–168. Provide a supply of red pens for correcting.

Using the Center

1. The student selects an activity sheet. The rule charts are provided as a resource if the student needs help.

2. Next, the student uses a red pen to mark corrections for each sentence on the activity sheet. How to proofread is modeled in the student directions.

3. Then the student copies each sentence correctly. The student evaluates the writing task using the checklist on the activity sheet.

4. Finally, the student checks the answers using the answer key.

Write It Right!

Correct the sentences with a red pen. The first one has been done for you. Copy the sentences correctly. Look at the answer key.

1. C̶an J̶im go to the circus with us?

   _____

   _____

2. pat and mike went to see scott

   _____

   _____

3. i can't believe we won the soccer game

   _____

   _____

4. do they live on maple street

   _____

   _____

✓ Check Your Work

- ○ I used a capital letter to begin each sentence.
- ○ I used a capital letter for names.
- ○ I used the correct mark at the end of each sentence.
- ○ I used a comma when it was needed.

Write It Right!

Correct the sentences with a red pen. The first one has been done for you. Copy the sentences correctly. Look at the answer key.

K   D   T
1. ~~k~~im took a trip to ~~d~~allas, ~~t~~exas.

_____

_____

2. will you put the toys away

_____

_____

3. i think halloween is so much fun

_____

_____

4. amy was born on june 6 1998

_____

_____

✔ **Check Your Work**

○ I used a capital letter to begin each sentence.
○ I used a capital letter for names.
○ I used the correct mark at the end of each sentence.
○ I used a comma when it was needed.

Name _____

Write It Right!

Correct the sentences with a red pen. The first one has been done for you. Copy the sentences correctly. Look at the answer key.

W
1. ~~w~~ho came to the party?

_____

_____

2. we hunt for eggs on easter sunday

_____

_____

3. it snows in january and february

_____

_____

4. sam and i stayed up all night long

_____

_____

✔ Check Your Work

- ○ I used a capital letter to begin each sentence.
- ○ I used a capital letter for names.
- ○ I used the correct mark at the end of each sentence.
- ○ I used a comma when it was needed.

Write It Right!

Write It Right!

Follow These Steps:

1. Read the Capital Letter Rules chart. Read the Punctuation Rules chart.

2. Take an activity sheet.

3. Use a red pen to correct the sentences. The first one has been done for you.

4. Copy the sentences correctly.

5. Check your work.

6. Look at the answer key to check your answers.

Writing Tips

It is easy to miss mistakes. That is why you have to check your writing very carefully. Checking for mistakes is called proofreading.

Be a proofreader. Check for the mistakes in the sentences. Find and fix the capitalization and punctuation mistakes.

Example

1. **Fix the mistakes.**

Laura and I like the month of December.

2. **Write the sentence correctly.**

Laura and I like the month of December.

Capital Letter Rules

Use a capital letter at the beginning of a sentence.	It is raining.
Use the capital letter **I** to name yourself.	Jane and I like pizza.

Use capital letters for names of people and places.

people's names	Sally Smith
street names	Elm Street
city names	Los Angeles
state names	Texas

Use capital letters for the days of the week and months of the year.

days of the week	Sunday
months of the year	March

Use capital letters for names of holidays.

holidays	Halloween

Punctuation Rules

Use a period (.) at the end of a sentence that tells something.	I went to the park.
Use a question mark (?) at the end of a sentence that asks something.	Did you go to the park?
Use an exclamation mark (!) to show strong feeling.	I love my new horse!
Use a comma (,) between a city and state name.	Dallas, Texas
Use a comma (,) in a date.	March 14, 2006

Write It Right!

Lift the flap to check your answers.

Write It Right! 1

1. C̶an J̶im go to the circus with us?

   Can Jim go to the circus with us?

2. P̶at and M̶ike went to see S̶cott.

   Pat and Mike went to see Scott.

3. I̶ can't believe we won the
   soccer game!

   I can't believe we won the
   soccer game!

4. D̶o they live on M̶aple S̶treet?

   Do they live on Maple Street?

Write It Right! 2

K   D   T
1. kim took a trip to dallas, texas.   Kim took a trip to Dallas, Texas.

W
2. will you put the toys away?   Will you put the toys away?

  I   H
3. i think halloween is so much fun!   I think Halloween is so much fun!

  A   J
4. amy was born on june 6, 1998.   Amy was born on June 6, 1998.

Write It Right! 3

W
1. who came to the party?   Who came to the party?

W
2. we hunt for eggs on   We hunt for eggs on
  E   S   Easter Sunday.
  easter sunday.

  I   J
3. it snows in january   It snows in January
       F   and February.
  and february.

  S   I
4. sam and i stayed   Sam and I stayed
  up all night long!   up all night long!

Pick a Story

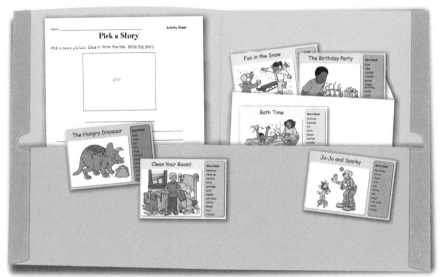

Task Cards

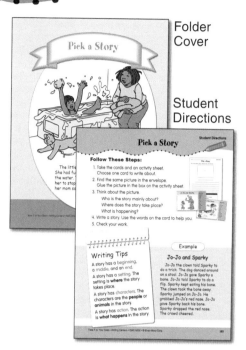

Folder Cover

Student Directions

Preparing the Center

1. Prepare a folder following the directions on page 3.

   Cover—page 183

   Student Directions—page 185

   Picture Cards—pages 187–191

2. Reproduce a supply of the activity sheet on page 180. Reproduce and cut apart a supply of the pictures on pages 181 and 182. Place these in an envelope in the folder.

Using the Center

1. The student selects a picture card and an activity sheet.

2. Next, the student finds the same picture in the envelope and glues it to the activity sheet.

3. Then the student writes a story about what is happening in the picture. A word bank is provided for student use. How to write a story is modeled in the student directions.

4. Finally, the student evaluates the writing task using the checklist on the activity sheet.

Pick a Story

Pick a story picture. Glue it. Write the title. Write the story.

```
┌─────────────────────────┐
│                         │
│                         │
│                         │
│          glue           │
│                         │
│                         │
│                         │
└─────────────────────────┘
```

_____

_____

_____

_____

_____

_____

_____

✔ Check Your Work

○ I wrote the title of the story.
○ My story tells about the main character.
○ My story tells about the setting.
○ My story tells what is happening.

Fun in the Snow

The Birthday Party

Jo-Jo and Sparky

Bath Time

The Hungry Dinosaur

Clean Your Room!

Pick a Story

Bath Time

The little girl had to take a bath. She had fun in the tub. She splashed in the water. The cat got wet. Her mom told her to stop making a mess. She did what her mom said. It was not as much fun.

Pick a Story

Follow These Steps:

1. Take the cards and an activity sheet.
   Choose one card to write about.

2. Find the same picture in the envelope.
   Glue the picture in the box on the activity sheet.

3. Think about the picture.

   Who is the story mainly about?
   Where does the story take place?
   What is happening?

4. Write a story. Use the words on the card to help you.

5. Check your work.

Writing Tips

A story has a beginning, a middle, and an end.

A story has a setting. The setting is **where** the story takes place.

A story has characters. The characters are the **people** or **animals** in the story.

A story has action. The action is **what happens** in the story.

Example

Jo-Jo and Sparky

Jo-Jo the clown told Sparky to do a trick. The dog danced around on a stool. Jo-Jo gave Sparky a bone. Jo-Jo told Sparky to do a flip. Sparky kept eating his bone. The clown took the bone away. Sparky jumped on Jo-Jo. He grabbed Jo-Jo's red nose. Jo-Jo gave Sparky back his bone. Sparky dropped the red nose. The crowd cheered.

Fun in the Snow

Word Bank

cold

earmuffs

gloves

play

scarf

sled

snow

snowball

snowing

snowman

throw

The Birthday Party

Word Bank

blow

cake

candles

friends

games

Happy
Birthday

invite

juice

party

presents

thank you

Pick a Story

© Evan-Moor Corp. • EMC 6002

Pick a Story

© Evan-Moor Corp. • EMC 6002

188   Take It to Your Seat—Writing Centers • EMC 6002 • © Evan-Moor Corp.

Jo-Jo and Sparky

Word Bank

big shoes
circus
clown
cute
dog
funny
hat
laugh
red nose
stool
tricks

Bath Time

Word Bank

bathtub
bubbles
cat
dirty
messy
mother
puddle
splash
sponge
towel
water

Pick a Story

Pick a Story

The Hungry Dinosaur

Word Bank

bush
chew
eat
feet
huge
hungry
large
leaves
long ago
nibble
scales
tail

Clean Your Room!

Word Bank

bedroom
clean up
clothes
dirty
garbage
junk
messy
put away
rotten
shoes
toys
trouble

Pick a Story

© Evan-Moor Corp. • EMC 6002

Pick a Story

© Evan-Moor Corp. • EMC 6002